From Burning to Blooming—A Journey Through Moods & Madness

Desiree Lozano

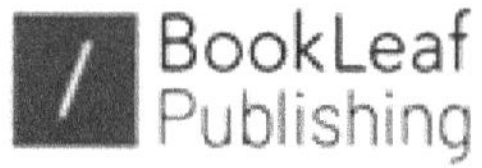

Presentation by *BookLeaf Publishing*

Web: www.bookleafpub.com

E-mail: info@bookleafpub.com

ISBN: 9789357211260

First edition 2022

DEDICATION

This book is dedicated to my best friend Elexie. She was, at times, my only guiding light as I walked through darkness.

Thank you my friend for the unconditional love you've always given me. You are my soul mate and I'm glad we found each other in this lifetime to experience this journey together. I know you understand these words better than anyone. I love you.

And to all the younger versions of myself. We did it and I'm so proud of you. Without you, our story wouldn't be told.

ACKNOWLEDGEMENT

This poetry book wouldn't be possible without the love and support from my family, friends and co-workers. Special thanks to my sister Christina who supports anything I do and is always there for me. As well as my niece and nephews, you all light up my whole world. Of course thank you to the friends I've made my family. Thank you for walking alongside me through this journey.

Finally, a very special thanks to BookLeaf Publishing for giving me this amazing opportunity to publish my work on their platform.

PREFACE

"Poetry comes from the highest happiness or the deepest sorrow."

Abdul Kalam

Welcome

Welcome to the inside of my head.
Where the sun illuminates the grassy hills of my
personality.
The flowers are in full bloom.
Vibrant in their colors and effervescent in their
energy.

A place where it's warm and welcoming.

But when the clouds roll in, they give no
warning.
My anger roars like thunder.
Words strike like lighting
while the rain drowns everything in sight.

Claircognizance

Being fluent
in the unspoken language
can be beautiful
yet crippling.

You'll always understand
what people are trying to tell you
without them speaking it into words,
as well as the things
they're trying not to tell you.

the message isn't in the words,
it's in the tone of their voice,
their body language,
their eye-contact.

The message is in the subtleties.
They give it all away.

My Apologies

When I apologize for my mess
I don't mean the clutter in my closet
or the stack of dishes in the sink.
I mean
the mess that is my mind,
the dark and intrusive thoughts that manifest
themselves into self-sabotaging behavior.
The dark hole filled with insecurities and fear of
uncertainty.
I mean
the mess that is conjured from a towering rage
that spew words like gunfire puncturing even the
thickest skin.

the mess that destroys everything in its path.

Please forgive me.

Practice Makes Perfect

It seems as if
I have mastered
the art of
resurrecting myself
back from the dead.
After all, you killed me
and here I am.
Now I just have to remember
how I managed
such sorcery.
'Cause this time, I killed me
and now
here I am.

The Graveyard

You are now part of the graveyard.
The graveyard of lost loves and perpetual
disappointments.
The graveyard of past friendships and old habits.
There is now a spot for you and the love we
shared.

I have to put you,
put us to rest
for you have moved on
and while this grave is meant for you

I was the one who died.

The Depression Hole

Looking back it was a blur of momentary
madness
And in between it nothing existed.

Falling into a deep hole of dark thoughts.
The chatter up above sounds muffled and
growing more distant.
Anything in my vision is blurry and sleep is the
only time I don't feel the weight of the pain.

All I think to myself is
"it's dark down here"
And normally I'd already be thinking of ways to
claw my way back up to the top but this time, I
think I'll sit.
Stay for a while.
I'm tired.

Grief

I thought I had never experienced grief

It wasn't until I lost my grandparents that grief
came knocking at my door.

Only, it didn't come for a short visit.
It was moving in.

Bringing all the baggage of my losses.
Suitcases of longing for my grandma and
grandpa.
Duffel bags of let downs and disappointments.
Garment bags with past versions of myself
hanging inside
and I can't forget the purse full of trauma and
triggers.

It wasn't until I started unpacking that I finally
realized what it truly meant. Grief.

After months of crying and shouting and
denying any part of it. I got up, wiped the tears
from my face, walked to the kitchen and made
two cups of coffee.

I sat down in front of grief slid over the cup of
coffee...and said.
"Stay as long as you need."

Drowning

These are the thoughts
that have me grasping
for breaths of freedom.
They sometimes quiet down
and the tide subsides
when I'm with a group of people.
But they're never forgotten
and when I'm alone it's like I'm in another
dimension
where all sounds are muffled out and my
thoughts take over,
they own me
own my body

own my time

and most importantly

my happiness.

Demons

We all have demons
I've known about mine for as long as I can
remember...
back to when I was a little girl even...
I didn't know what to do with them then,
perhaps I didn't even know what they were
but
as I've gotten older I've developed a deeper
understanding of my demons...as well as having
created new ones with age.
I've learned to not only acknowledge their
existence but how to sit face to face with each
one individually and dig into why they haunt me
so.
I learned where they originated from and asked
them to show me the ways of my subconscious.
As uncomfortable and excruciatingly painful as
the process was I was able to develop a new
found friendship with my demons.
They've taught me a lot about myself, about
others, about those I've loved, about those I
thought I loved.

they are a part of who I am,
and I'm okay with that

They exist
sometimes they're with me
and
sometimes they're against me.

but either way
they're just passengers
I'm the one driving the car.

What Was Left

When depression moved in, it completely took
over.
I was too little to claim my space. I let it turn a
vibrant home full of magic into a space of
darkness.

It resided in my body for a while,
It's best friends we're shame and anger who
made frequent visits.

As I got older and slowly began to reclaim what
was rightfully mine...

I didn't feel like I was in my body anymore.
What was left was a hollow shell of a body
where a human used to be.
Depression had taken all my magic and turned it
into darkness.
Who was I?
Learning to love myself was like re-building my
home from the ground up.
Piece by piece.

The Files of Us

Sometimes I grab the file of us
and I scatter the memories
all over the table.

They lay there, faded and dusty,
out of order,
cut and cropped.

I open the file because I need to see they still
exist.
The memories of us.
To remember existing within those memories
to remember myself falling in love for the first
time
to remember the euphoric high highs and
ohh to remember the devastatingly low lows.

To remember thinking I'd never feel this way
again
and to remember myself surviving it all.

I then place those memories back in the folder
and file it away deep in my past
where it belongs.

Just Write

Words are my favorite things in the world.
We are in an intimate relationship words and I.
Reading them...writing them,
the way they can draw every type of emotion.
26 letters yet endless possibilities.
Letters strung together to create an infinite world
of words,
words that can express love and adoration,
and words that utter cruelty and heartbreak.

Writing has allowed me to put my pain to down
into words,
to dance with the emotions and put them down
on paper.

So whenever my heart is heavy and my mind is
busy,
I hear it tell me
just write.

Reminder

Above all else
please remember
that everything will get better,
maybe not today
maybe not even tomorrow
or next week
but you'll wake up one day
and it won't be so heavy.
It won't be the first thing you think of
before you even open your eyes
and you'll know.

Love Language

I am learning
my own love language
through all the ways
I broke myself
trying to
p i e c e
together
someone else.

Unconditional Love

I handed over my heart to you.
Battered and full of scars.
Ready for you to exile me like all the others
but you didn't.
You took it into your hands and caressed each
scar with your gentle touch.

You have found all the dark, dusty corners.
Corners I never thought would see light again.
You found them
dusted them out
planted flowers
and your love is the light illuminating growth.

Road to Self-Love

The journey to self love has proven to be a
lonely one,
But every step of the way has been worth it.
I feel myself blooming like the flowers in the
spring with those warm rays of sunshine
beaming down on my face only this time the
light is radiating from within.

Every milestone of progress makes me crave
more and i've become curious about what else I
can achieve on this journey.

Regardless if i'm a blooming flower on a warm
summer day or a fallen leaf on a cold autumn
morning, like the seasons I too will change and
the love for myself will remain.

Your Influence

One glance
& I go weak in the knees.
one glance and the words from my poetry start
spewing out of me like a bad hangover.

Museum of Me

I used to think my complexities made me a work
of art
until I realized,
I was the whole damn museum.

My past tells stories throughout different
exhibits,

The shattered pieces of my heart on display up
above,
creating a kaleidoscope of colors.
Delicate, intricate, well thought-out yet
beautifully messy.

The walls filled with the scars from my demons,
Intricate and textured.
Each one tells you their story and how they were
formed
Some cuts go deep while others go dark.

The last few rooms are still empty as the artist
finishes her collections.

I Love My love

I spent my whole life allowing others to burn out
my flame because it was too bright for them.
I even became an expert at extinguishing it
myself in consideration of others.
With only a faint spark illuminating, I reignited
my flame over and over again.
Getting better at it every time and now who ever
gets too close risks getting burned.
Rising from the ashes bigger and brighter than
the last,
You'll never put out my flame again.

I Am Magic

There is a light that has always been inside of
me,
yet others have always tried to extinguish it.
Any sight of it gleaming would quickly be
turned out
for it burned too bright for their liking.
Until finally, that light was down to just a faint
glimmer.

After spending much time in darkness, that
glimmer was the only illumination I had.
The longer I stayed, the brighter it got and it
shed light on on who I truly am.
I have mastered the art of reigniting my spark
and over again.

That's my magic.

Like-Minds

If you are to write to a specific person
write to the one who
unknowingly follows
in your footsteps.
to the one who loves to break their own heart
by means of self-destruction & chaos of the
mind
& tell them
Hey, don't overthink everything.
Embrace the good times when you have them
and take care of yourself in the bad times.
'Cause trust me when I say
it doesn't last forever.
and hey,
whatever you do
please do not indulge yourself in
destructive thought
you will only burn out your own flame.